The Horrific Crimes of Gilles de Rais Revisited

Copyrights

All rights reserved. © Jack Smith and Maplewood Publishing. No part of this publication or the information in it may be quoted from or reproduced in any form by means such as printing, scanning, photocopying, or otherwise without prior written permission of the copyright holder.

Disclaimer and Terms of Use

Effort has been made to ensure that the information in this book is accurate and complete. However, the author and the publisher do not warrant the accuracy of the information, text, and graphics contained within the book due to the rapidly changing nature of science, research, known and unknown facts, and internet. The author and the publisher do not hold any responsibility for errors, omissions, or contrary interpretation of the subject matter herein. This book is presented solely for motivational and informational purposes only.

Warning

Throughout the book there are some descriptions of murders and crime scenes that some people might find disturbing

ISBN-13: 978-1530142958
ISBN-10: 1530142954

Printed in the Unites States

The Horrific Crimes of Gilles de Rais Revisited

Life of a Serial Killer of the Middle Ages

Jack Smith

Contents

Introduction _____ 1
Childhood _____ 13
Blood Feuds _____ 19
Killer Precedents _____ 29
The Maid of Orleans _____ 39
Fall from Grace _____ 47
Black Magic _____ 57
Double Jeopardy _____ 66
Arrested _____ 72
Guilty _____ 78
Aftermath _____ 84
Conclusion _____ 89
Bibliography _____ 95
Photography Credits _____ 97
More Books from Jack Smith _____ 99

Introduction

La Roche-Bernard, France. September, 1438

Peronne Loessart knew that she should feel honored, both for herself and on her young son's behalf. But she was still in a state of unease bordering on fear.

The Baron de Rais and his entourage were in her town, stopping at the hotel of Jean Colin, which was in the immediate neighborhood of Madame Loessart's home. One of the Baron's men, a man named Poitou, had spied her ten-year-old son and approached her about engaging the boy as his page.

Young Loessart often drew such attention. He was an uncommonly beautiful child, with golden hair and expressive blue eyes. But this was the first time that he had come to the notice of a potential patron.

Poitou, whose real name was Étienne Corrillaut, went to Madame Loessart and offered her four pounds for the boy's services, with an added bonus of one hundred *sous* for a new dress. He also promised to continue the child's education at a prestigious institution.

Although distressed at the thought of being parted from her son, Madame Loessart finally agreed. She knew that he had limited opportunities for advancement in La Roche-Bernard. Poitou also gave her his word that the boy would be well provided for.

She believed it. Gilles de Rais was the Marshal of France, a great man who had helped Jeanne d'Arc bring about the victory at Orléans. A regal escort preceded him wherever he went and trumpeters announced his presence at each destination. His ostentatious display of wealth and pageantry turned heads and inspired both awe and adoration. Now her son would have the chance to benefit from such glory.

A pony was purchased from the hotel owner for the boy to ride, and the Baron's entourage left for his castle at Machecoul the following day. There was probably a tearful goodbye, accompanied by promises to send messages and see each other soon.

Despite the excellent opportunity she appeared to be giving her son, Madame Loessart remained anxious. Perhaps separation anxiety was taking hold. Maybe the rumors that had been circulating lately now seemed more plausible. Whatever the reason, she suddenly ran after the departing party.

One of the Baron's servants intercepted the distraught woman and held her back, reminding her that a bargain had been struck. Gilles de Rais did not respond to her pleas. Instead, he spoke to the servant restraining her.

"He (the child) is well chosen. He is as beautiful as an angel."

Finally Madame Loessart calmed down, and the Baron's party resumed its journey.

Two years passed. The Baron's servants passed through the village once during that time, although young Loessart was not with them. On demanding news of her son, the men informed her that the boy was either at Tiffauges or Pouzauges. The truth was that he was long dead.

******

If the Loessart boy's fate was typical (at least according to later testimony), he was taken to one of Gilles de Rais' castles, given a perfumed bath, and dressed in better clothes than he had ever worn. That evening, after a sumptuous meal and plenty of hippocras[1], his keepers brought him to an upstairs room that only Rais and his

---

[1] A spice-laden heated wine, which was consumed as a stimulant

inner circle had access to. There his keepers bluntly informed him of what lay ahead. The boy's shock and fear served as an aphrodisiac for Rais, exciting him into violence the way that the smell of blood inspires a predator.

Étienne Corrillaut, alias Poitou, was a self-confessed accomplice in many of the murders. He later testified that his master started many of these "sessions" by hanging his victims from a hook to keep them from crying out and then masturbating upon the child's belly or thighs. He would then take the boy down, comfort him, and insist he was only "playing". But what followed next was far from playful. After the games ended, Rais either killed the child himself or designated the task to his cousin Gilles de Sillé, Poitou, or another manservant named Henriet Griert.

This alleged period of rampage and murder coincided with a serious decline in Gilles de Rais' personal fortune. After his military service concluded, he sank money into a series of extravagances: the construction of an opulent chapel (called, ironically, the Chapel of the Holy Innocents) and a theatrical spectacle titled *Le Mistère du Siège d'Orléans*, which featured over 600 costumes and unlimited food and drink for the audience. Alarmed, his family persuaded King Charles VII to intervene, resulting in a royal edict that forbade Rais from selling any more property.[2]

Desperate to restore his fortune, he embraced alchemy and invoked demons to intervene, an arrangement that author Joris-Karl Huysmans called "the chemical coitus." In 1439, he engaged Italian former cleric François Prelati to summon a demon named Barron, who could produce gold.

Prelati fed him stories about Barron wanting sacrifices before providing assistance. The Italian later swore to a panel of judges that Rais offered the hearts, eyes, and sexual organs of his small victims to appease the demon. Predictably, there was no result.

Strangely, despite the murders, rapes, and desecrations he had allegedly committed, Gilles de Rais considered himself a devout Catholic. Huysmans commented, "He carried his zeal for prayer in the territory of blasphemy." When frightened, he would cross himself or entreat God. During his last moments, he continued to believe that he and his accomplices were destined for heaven.

******

---

[2] Benedetti, Jean. *Gilles de Rais*, p.135

Gilles de Rais is purportedly history's most infamous sexual serial murderer. He was accused of the mutilation, rape, and murder of more than 150 boys and girls, although it was rumored for years afterward that the final victim count could have been as high as 800. The record for his trial is one of the best-documented cases of serial murder during the Middle Ages.

Before his alleged deeds were discovered, Gilles de Rais enjoyed both prestige and power. He became Marshal of France at the age of 24, owned large estates, and basked in the glow of an illustrious military career, having been one of France's most active generals in the Hundred Years War. But an extravagant and wasteful lifestyle led him to financial ruin, and his declared lust for innocent blood led him to the gallows.

Legend claimed that whenever he needed fresh victims, Rais would send his most trusted servants out to the villages and countryside to find beautiful children and bring them back. He preferred boys, but settled for girls when no alternative existed. These servants said that once the children were in the castle, a night of lusty mayhem began that ended in murder.

This was an era when there was practically no limit to the power of French feudal lords like Gilles de Rais. He and his contemporaries could theoretically torture or kill subordinates on a whim, without fear of intervention by the King. In what has to be a classic example of power-obsessed hypocrisy, the Catholic Church tolerated such abuses as long as heresy did not creep into the picture, as heresy was a direct threat to the Church's own power. When Catholic authorities heard rumors that the Baron was practicing black magic to influence his declining fortunes, they moved in.

At his trial, Rais reacted to threats of torture and excommunication by making a full confession and corroborating the stories of his co-conspirators. He and his attendants "inflicted various types and manners of torment," he said. Afterward, he disposed of his victims by strangling them, smashing their heads in with a blunt instrument, or hanging them from a hook in his room. As their lives ebbed away, he would "commit the sodomitic vice on them," and keep going even after they died. If the child were especially handsome, he would decapitate them and keep the head for a while afterward, lavishing it with kisses.

Hearing such testimony, the anguish of Peronne Loessart and the mothers of his other victims must have been unspeakable. They had long hesitated to speak out against a nobleman, knowing that their words – and their lives – would be valueless compared to his. Now, shielded – and, some would say, coached – by the Catholic Church, they banded together to bring him down.

After the ecclesiastical court condemned him and his servants, Poitou and Henriet, to death, Rais made a request to die first, so that he might serve as an example to his co-conspirators. It was granted, and later writers like Georges Bataille held this up as an example of the Baron's amoral exhibitionism. Rais had been obsessed with pageantry and spectacle, and Bataille claimed that the thought of everyone being able to watch his hanging, burning body allowed Gilles de Rais to exit the earthly plane with the same sense of violent theater that accompanied his existence.

******

Centuries later, the question persists, like a blemish on French history that refuses to go away.

Did he do it?

Did Gilles de Rais really massacre hundreds of children undetected before the Church and the citizenry joined forces to stop and punish him?

Aleister Crowley delivered a series of lectures on Gilles de Rais and his alleged crimes at Oxford University in 1930. Crowley believed that the murders were exaggerations at best and outright fabrications at worst. His position was that Gilles de Rais had been targeted and victimized by the Catholic Church.

"He was accused of the same crimes as Joan of Arc by the same people who accused her, and that he was condemned by them to the same penalty," he argued.

The real problem of Gilles de Rais amounts, accordingly, to this. Here we have a person who, in almost every respect, was the male equivalent of Joan of Arc. Both of them have gone down in history. But history is somewhat curious. I am still inclined to think that "there ain't no such animal." In the time of Shakespeare, Joan of Arc was accepted in England as a symbol for everything vile. He makes her out not only as a sorceress, but a charlatan and hypocrite; and on top of that a coward, a liar, and a common slut. I suspect that they began to whitewash her when they decided that she was a virgin, that is a sexually deranged, or at least incomplete, animal, but the idea has always got people going, as any student of religion knows. Anyway, her stock went up to the point of canonization. Gilles de Rais, on the other hand, is equally a household work for monstrous vices and crimes. So much so, that his is even confused with the fabulous figure of Bluebeard, of whom, even were he real, we know nothing much beyond that he reacted in the most manly way to the problem of domestic infelicity.

Others have pointed out that the Duke of Brittany, who brought forth charges for the secular proceedings that accompanied the ecclesiastical ones, received title to the Baron's lands after his conviction. When the Duke started dividing the properties among his own nobles before the verdict was even announced, there were mutterings that the French state framed Rais to seize his assets.

The debate remains, but the general consensus is that Gilles de Rais was a dedicated hedonist whose destructive habits consumed his wealth, destroyed his heroic legacy, and ended scores of lives. As Jason DeBoer wrote in his essay *Blood, Fuck, God: The Prodigal Crimes of Gilles de Rais*, "These medieval crimes still resonate today as hideous, self-negating acts, as the strange gestures of a nobleman and hero transformed by his own ruinous desires into a wastrel and murderer."[3]

---

[3] http://www.absintheliteraryreview.com/archives/fierce9.htm

"Gilles de Rais" by Éloi Firmin Féron

Childhood

Gilles de Rais was born in September or October 1404 to Guy II de Montmorency-Laval and Marie de Craon in the family castle at Champtocé-sur-Loire, around 12 miles west of Angers. His baptism was attended by members of the nobility from the surrounding regions, each one bearing a candle. Given the baby's ancestral connection to some of the most illustrious houses in medieval France, this sign of respect and honor was expected.

His father, Guy II de Montmorency-Laval, knight and Lord of Blaison and Chemillé, was descended from the Montmorencys, who were the first Barons of France. Marie de Craon, his mother, was a direct descendant of King Robert II (972-1031). (Ironically, history has credited Robert with restoring the imperial Roman custom of burning heretics at the stake, legitimizing the mode of the execution imposed on Gilles and his associates four hundred years later.[4]) Marie de Craon also claimed kinship to the opulent houses of Machecoul and Rais, ensuring that Gilles and his younger brother René stood to inherit immense wealth.

---

[4] MacCulloch, Diarmaid. *A History of Christianity*. Penguin Books, 2010, p. 396

Like most unions among thirteenth century French nobility, the marriage of Gilles de Rais' parents had been politically motivated. It was also the result of more greed, hatred, and intrigue than a modern soap opera.

******

In 1371, the last Baron of Rais, Chabot V, died without an heir, passing the ancient house to his sister Jeanne, who was also known as "Jeanne la Sage (Sensible)." She too was childless, and in casting about for a successor, decided on her younger cousin Guy II de Montmorency-Laval.

There was a problem, however: Guy's grandmother, "Crazy" Jeanne (Jeanne la Folle) of Rais, had been disinherited after marrying for love, and the decree blocked the rights of her descendants to the Barony of Rais.

With her customary shrewdness, Jeanne la Sage got around that obstacle by offering to adopt her cousin and legally include him in her family line. There was only one condition: Guy II de Montmorency-Laval had to renounce the title and arms of Laval and assume those of the house of Rais. On September 23, 1401, he agreed, and the adoption was formalized.

The family harmony was short-lived. For some reason, Jeanne and her new heir soon had an irreparable argument. She canceled their arrangement and chose another successor, Catherine de Machecoul, who was also a distant cousin. Madame de Machecoul was a widow with a son, Jean de Craon, who now stood to become Baron of Rais under the new arrangement.

Furious, Guy initiated a lawsuit before the Parliament of Paris. The bitter legal battle went on for years. Both sides finally reached a compromise: if Guy married Jean de Craon's daughter, Marie, the barony of Rais would be his. He agreed, and the wedding was duly celebrated on February 5, 1404. Two years after the couple's first child, Gilles, was born, Jeanne la Sage died, and Guy II de Montmorency-Laval officially became the Baron de Rais.

******

Seal of Guy de Rais

Gilles was a child of above-average intelligence. He spoke Latin fluently, which was a sign of breeding and high station in medieval France, and was a voracious reader. As a grown man, with his dark hair, pale skin, and lithe but powerful form, he cut a figure that contemporaries described as "angelic."

For an individual who was exposed as a sadist in his twenties, Gilles had a relatively benign childhood. He was spoiled and entitled, as were most children of the nobility during that era, but there was no evidence of abnormal behavior during his boyhood, and he committed no known battlefield cruelties during his campaigns against the English during the revival of the Hundred Years War. Had the case been otherwise, it would have been recalled and remarked upon after the child murders came to light.

Eminent crime historian Colin Wilson compared Gilles de Rais to mass murderers like Vlad III, Prince of Wallachia (also known as Vlad the Impaler) and Ivan IV Vasilyevich, more commonly known as Ivan the Terrible. Both men were infamous for their juvenile cruelty: Vlad was especially brutal after the Turks took him prisoner during his teenage years, and Ivan was a bully and sadist who delighted in tormenting anyone too weak to fight back.

Gilles does not appear to have experienced any similar traumas or personality disorders that foreshadowed a serial killer.

Wilson wrote, "Gilles' attacks of sadism seem to have descended on him like an epileptic fit." The Baron's purported latent sadism does defy explanation because his early years contained no warning signs. Even H.G. Wells, who commented on his crimes in a book called *Crux Ansata*, ultimately pronounced him "unanalyzable." Yet when he was accused of multiple murders, his judges – and history – have accepted his guilt completely.

Blood Feuds

On September 28, 1415, Guy II de Montmorency-Laval died in what has been described as a "gory hunting accident."[5] His death made his oldest son Gilles the Baron de Rais and heir to one of France's most magnificent fortunes. Rais was the senior barony of Brittany, bordered by Loire on the north, on the west by the Atlantic Ocean, and Lac de Grandlieu and Poitou to the east and south respectively. From his father and grandfather, he would also inherit lands and lordships in Anjou and the surrounding regions.

The fate of Marie de Craon is less certain. According to some accounts, she died shortly before her husband. Other sources claim that soon after the death of her husband she married again, this time to Charles d'Estouteville, Lord of Villebon. In either case, she disappeared from her sons' lives, and their guardianship passed to her father, Jean de Craon.

Craon, who might have inherited the barony himself had Guy II de Montmorency-Laval not agreed to marry his only daughter, was getting on in years. At his trial, Gilles would say that his grandfather was overly indulgent,

---

[5] Villalon, L. J. Andrew. *The Hundred Years War (Part III): Further Considerations*, p.146

letting both of his young wards get away with outrageous behavior. Free of boundaries, Gilles became accustomed to getting what he wanted when he wanted it, leading to impatience with delayed gratification and a lack of regard for others.

Although Jean de Craon may not have supervised his grandsons closely, he tirelessly schemed for the advancement of Gilles in particular. On October 25, 1415 Craon's only son, Amaury, was killed at the Battle of Agincourt, which was a disastrous defeat for France. Now Gilles stood to inherit the vast Craon wealth too.

In 1416, Craon arranged a future match between the twelve-year-old boy and four-year-old Jeanne Paynel, one of the wealthiest heiresses in Normandy. The two were betrothed in January 1417, but the plan fell through when Jeanne died after a brief illness. Next, Craon proposed a union between Gilles and Béatrice de Rohan, the niece to the Duke of Brittany, but she died too.

Although child mortality was high in medieval France, the deaths of Jeanne and Béatrice helped form the basis of the claim that Gilles de Rais was the original Bluebeard, the villain in Charles Perrault's famous French folktale. The story chronicles a depraved and violent nobleman who murders one wife after another, a spree that has no resemblance to Rais' alleged crimes except the high victim count.

Craon called a temporary halt to the matchmaking. By 1420, war was on the horizon in their region of France, and his grandson was provided with a different opportunity to honor the family name.

******

The Breton War of Succession, which raged from 1341 until 1364, had been a struggle between the Montforts of Brittany and the Counts of Blois for control of the Duchy of Brittany. The slaughter levels were horrific: when Charles of Blois overran the city of Quimper in May 1344, an estimated 1400 to 2000 civilians were massacred. Breton and Norman prisoners were sent to Paris where they were executed for treason.

The Montforts prevailed, and a diplomatic treaty was signed, but in the years following the war, the defeated Blois faction continued to plot their comeback. Finally, in February 1420, Olivier de Blois, Count of Penthièvre, reopened the conflict by kidnapping Jean V, the ruling Duke of Brittany.

Jean de Craon and sixteen-year-old Gilles took the side of the kidnapped Duke and the House of Montfort. The Count of Penthièvre sent bands of thugs into the Craon and Rais territories, where they spread terror. Coming from a family of medieval knights, and trained as a soldier after he entered his teens, Gilles fought back with a fierceness that belied his youth. He killed some of the assailants and put the others on the run, exhilarated by the raw violence of combat. Rais also helped his grandfather secure the release of Jean V.

The grateful Duke of Brittany compensated them both for the losses inflicted by enemy marauders and granted them portions of land seized from the Penthièvres. He also gave them an annuity of one hundred pounds.[6]

Fortified by new wealth, Gilles and his grandfather returned their attention to his matrimonial situation, which was yet another way to increase the family fortune. The young Rais set his eyes on – and some said took by force – the beautiful and wealthy Catherine de Thouars of Brittany, heiress of La Vendée and Poitou.

******

---

[6] Approximately eight million dollars in 2015.

Other than the fact that she was the daughter of Milet de Thouars, Lord of Pouzauges and Tiffauges, and Béatrice de Montjean and had vast holdings in Poitou, which adjoined the Barony of Rais, little is known about Catherine at this time. She and Gilles were first cousins, which required a marriage union to be approved by the Church beforehand. Her father also opposed the idea of a match, insisting that they were too closely related.

Catherine's parents later claimed that Gilles de Rais abducted their daughter and forced her to marry him, which is unlikely given the fact that she remained with him willingly afterward and supported his later schemes against her own family. Milet de Thouars attempted to have the marriage dissolved on the grounds of consanguinity, but died of a fever before he could succeed.

Gilles and his grandfather greedily took possession of Catherine's lands and estates, as well as the Thouars-owned fortresses at Tiffauges and Pouzauges. That same year, Jean de Craon's wife died, and he married Anne de Sillé, Catherine's widowed grandmother, further strengthening the ties between the two families. Her grandson, Gilles de Sillé, would one day be an enthusiastic participant in the child murders.

Béatrice de Montjean was unable to fight back until the following year, when she married Jacques Meschin de la Roche-Airault, a knight who had been chamberlain in the Dauphin's[7] court. When papal authorities in Rome formally approved the marriage of Gilles and Catherine, Meschin approached the couple and demanded the return of certain seized lands, saying they were part of his wife's dowry instead.

It was a serious mistake on his part. In 1423, Gilles and Jean de Craon kidnapped Béatrice de Montjean and her younger sister and imprisoned them at Champtocé, one of Craon's holdings. They told her that unless she renounced her claim to Tiffauges and Pouzauges, allowing Gilles to own them through Catherine, she would be sewn in a sack and thrown in the river. The same message was conveyed to her husband, Jacques Meschin. To compound the threat, Jean de Craon abducted three of Meschin's men, including his brother Gilles Meschin, and threw them into a deep pit.

Craon's wife, Anne de Sillé, (who was also Béatrice de Montjean's mother) persuaded him to eventually release Béatrice, but Meschin had to pay a ransom to recover his brother and the other two men from the pit. Gilles Meschin died soon afterward from his injuries.

---

[7] In France's royal hierarchy, a Dauphin was the heir to the throne

Desperate and terrorized, Jacques de Meschin brought the matter before the royal parliament. For whatever reason, the kidnapping of Béatrice and death of Gilles Meschin were not addressed during the proceedings: the sole focus was on the lands that Gilles de Rais had seized and which Meschin insisted were part of his wife's dowry. A settlement was reached that restored some of Béatrice de Montjean's property to her, but when Adam de Cambrai, President of France's Parliament, came to Gilles and Catherine de Rais' fortress at Pouzauges to see the settlement signed, Jean de Craon and Gilles had him brutally assaulted.

This bold act of defiance resulted in a heavy fine being levied against Craon and Rais, but they ignored it. Royal influence had been seriously weakened by the Agincourt defeat in 1415, so like most feudal lords who knew that the monarchy relied on them for military support, they did what they wanted and got away with it. In 1443, three years after Gilles died, both fines remained unpaid.

******

In 1425, after Gilles de Rais had attained his majority and assumed administration of his lands, he was formally presented at the court of the Dauphin (the future King Charles VII). His good looks and ability to assume courtly manners when it suited him earned royal attention and favor. From 1427 to 1435, Rais was a commander in the Royal Army, distinguishing himself by displaying bravery on the battlefield when the Hundred Years War sprang back to life. One of his more notable accomplishments was the capture of the English captain Blackburn at the battle for the Château of Lude.

It was probably during his time at court (and away from his wife) that Gilles began to indulge his homosexuality. His favorite books included the works of Suetonius, which detailed the sexual excesses and depravities of the Roman emperors. He admitted at his trial that these stories fueled his fantasies and inspired a taste for the forbidden.

His marital relationship ebbed accordingly. Gilles and Catherine's only child, Marie, was born in 1429. Afterward, the couple was rarely together, but like most men of power, Gilles did not lack for sexual companionship. In 1427 he engaged ten-year-old Étienne Corrillaut as a page. Master and servant were uncommonly – some said unnaturally – close. Corrillaut, who went by the nickname Poitou, became Gilles' valet once old enough to do so. In addition to being his master's lover, he would actively recruit child victims and help kill them afterward.

Years later, Poitou told the ecclesiastical tribunal that his master assaulted him and threatened to kill him with a dagger not long after he entered the latter's service, but he was spared because of his good looks. This testimony, which supported the prosecutor's contention that the murders started in 1426, may or may not have been the result of torture, but it certainly came in handy when Jean de Malestroit, Bishop of Nantes, wanted to portray one of France's greatest war heroes as a degenerate by asserting that she knowingly acted as the consort of a sodomite and murderer.

Her name was Jeanne d'Arc.

Killer Precedents

Although the alleged crimes of Gilles de Rais were shocking enough to be remembered centuries later, he was not history's first mass murderer. While relatively uncommon, serial killing has been a phenomenon since the beginning of time.

One of the earliest recorded instances of multiple murder took place around 331 BC in Ancient Rome. Several Roman men who also happened to be members of the Senate suddenly fell ill with plague-like symptoms and died. They were assumed to be victims of an epidemic until a servant woman came to the aedile, which was responsible for maintaining public order, and revealed that they were actually victims of foul play.

Upon being granted immunity, the girl said that a "conspiracy of matrons" was behind the deaths, which were due to poison. She volunteered to show the officials where the concoctions were being made, and led the men to a house where a number of women were found brewing poisons. These mixtures were brought into the Forum, along with twenty married women who had been implicated.

Two of these women, Cornelia and Sergia, insisted that the mixtures were medicinal, and intended to combat the epidemic. The informer servant challenged them to drink the concoctions and prove her wrong in front of everyone. The two noblewomen, after conferring with their accused co-conspirators, finally agreed. Moments after drinking the potion, they perished.

The attendants of the accused women were promptly arrested. These frightened slaves informed against even more matrons, of whom 170 were later found guilty and executed.[8] Roman authorities, anxious to downplay the idea that women could cunningly band together to take down their masters, dismissed the murders as acts of madness rather than criminal intelligence.

******

Nearly 400 years later, the canonical first solo serial killer appeared. This new "fiend" was also female, and she operated in Rome.

Locusta was born in Gaul, one of the outer Roman provinces (now France). During her youth in the countryside, she acquired an in-depth knowledge of

---

[8] DONNE, William Mowbray. *C. Sallustii Crispi Catilina Et Bellum Jugurthinum ... With Notes by W.M. Donne*, p.133

herbs and plants, namely which ones healed and which ones could kill.

When she arrived in Rome, Locusta soon saw that ambitious, greedy people were everywhere. Some of them wanted their political rivals and rich relatives dead so badly that they were willing to pay for a discreet, accomplished murder. Locusta cashed in on these malevolent intentions by becoming a professional poisoner.

After her first successful assassinations, her reputation spread and she was rarely lacking for clients. Although arrested often for her activities, Locusta's influential customers always came to her aid and secured her release.

In 54 AD, the Empress Agrippina, wife of Emperor Claudius, secretly summoned the celebrated poisoner. She wanted Nero, her son from an earlier marriage, to become Emperor, and to realize that ambition, Claudius had to die. Locusta obliged by arranging for the 64-year-old Emperor to eat poisoned mushrooms, clearing Nero's path to the top.
Almost.

Claudius's other son, Britannicus, challenged Nero's right to become Emperor and laid claim to the throne. The worried new Emperor secured Locusta's release from prison where she had been sent for poisoning another victim, and even set her up in a large estate where students were sent to learn the art of murder. She reciprocated by poisoning Britannicus' wine.

Business boomed thereafter. Things were good for Locusta until Nero committed suicide. In 69 AD, his successor, Emperor Galba, held the murderess accountable for all the lives she had taken. After being chained and led through the streets of Rome, she was put to death on January 8.

If legend is to be believed, Locusta's execution was brutal even by Ancient Roman standards. After being raped by a specially trained giraffe, she was ripped apart by wild animals while a cheering public looked on. Historians later challenged this allegation, but January 8 was also the Agonalia festival, and bestiality was a routine entertainment at these events. Although horrible to contemplate, Rome's most notorious murderer could actually have died this way.

******

Although the twentieth century media made a huge deal over the possibility that Prince Albert Victor, the Duke of Clarence, could have been Jack the Ripper, a serial killer of royal blood was not new. From 144-116 BC in Imperial China, a rogue prince murdered over a hundred civilians.

Liu Pengli was the Prince of Jidong during the reign of his uncle, Emperor Jing. The black sheep of an otherwise illustrious family, he assembled groups of violent slaves and set forth at night on murdering, raping, and robbing expeditions. Jidong residents lived in fear of him, locking themselves in their homes at night and refraining from going out after dark.

By the time the authorities stopped the mayhem, Pengli had killed or ordered the killing of over a hundred people. The Chinese court recommended his execution, but the Emperor recoiled from the thought of putting a prince to death, and instead reduced him to a common Chinese subject and exiled him to Shangyong in modern Zhushan County, Hubei Province. If he continued to kill as a commoner, details of the murders were not preserved for posterity.

******

The next serial murder of note was also of noble blood, so by the time Gilles de Rais faced his judges, rogue nobility was not a unique phenomenon.

Queen Anula of Anuradhapura Kingdom (Sri Lanka) could have been remembered for more praiseworthy accomplishments. She was the first woman in the country's history to wield genuine power and authority. During her reign (50-47 BC), she was Asia's first female head of state. But these milestones could not whitewash the fact that she was an evil woman who killed for both pleasure and gain.[9]

Anula's husband, King Chora Naga (63-51 BC), had the unenviable distinction of being her first victim. She poisoned him so that her lover, Siva, could become king while she remained the actual power behind the throne. But before Siva could be crowned, a Sinhalese claimant named Kuda Tissa, the son of Chora Naga's predecessor, moved in. Anula swallowed her resentment and married him, but after a year and four months Tissa mysteriously died of fever-like symptoms. Siva now became king with no opposition.

---

[9] http://unknownmisandry.blogspot.ca/2011/09/anula-of-anuradhapura-sri-lankan-black.html

Anula soon tired of Siva. Perhaps he stopped taking direction from her, or maybe she felt that her new paramour, a Tamil named Vatuka, would be a more malleable monarch. Whatever the reason, fourteen months later, King Siva fell ill with severe stomach pains. He gasped for breath, vomited blood, and complained that his stomach burned. After he died, poisoning may have been suspected, but no one apparently connected the deed to Anula, who must have thrilled with accomplishment after Vatuka was crowned king.

The Tamil monarch lasted just over a year. Then he too, died under mysterious circumstances and a Purohita Brahmin advisor named Neeliya came to power. Anula, who had been sleeping with him for months, remained at his side as queen for the six months that he occupied the throne. Then he joined the growing ranks of murdered kings.

Anula went through two more royal lovers, Vdsukifor and Bela Tissa. Then she decided that she could do a better job than any of her previous masters and ruled the country herself for four months.

Perhaps the thought of an autonomous queen alarmed the authorities more than the years of regicide. Kutakanna Tissa, brother of the murdered Kuda Tissa, deposed Anula and had her arrested. She was supposedly executed by immolation (burning), either on a funeral pyre or within the palace where she had committed her crimes.

******

Queen Anula's ashes had been cool for over five hundred years when the next serial killer of note appeared. Zu Shenatir, a nobleman residing in fifth century El-Yemen, had an insatiable lust for young men and boys. He would entice them into his palace, rape them repeatedly, and then toss them to their deaths out of upper-level windows. It was one of his victims, not the authorities, who stopped him: a youth named Zerash fought back and succeeded in stabbing him to death.

******

Prior to the trial and execution of Gilles de Rais, Europe's last serial killer was Alice Kyteler, otherwise known as the "witch of Kilkenny." She came from a wealthy and powerful family, and had influential enemies as well as friends.

Alice's first husband was a moneylender named William Outlawe (Utlagh). He died not too long after marrying her. So did two more husbands, which aroused local suspicions even during an era of rampant disease and high mortality rates.

When her last husband, John Le Poer fell gravely ill and Alice set herself up as the sole beneficiary of his estate, gossip escalated into outright accusation. Doctors were unable to determine what was causing Le Poer to burn inside and waste away, and with his children from a previous marriage robbed of their inheritance, he began doubting his wife's integrity.

According to legend, Le Poer and his grown children travelled to Alice Kyteler's home by the sea and found items that smacked of witchcraft. The catalogue of items varies from one version of the story to the next, but they include candles made from human fat, infant body parts, communion wafers with satanic images, and powders that presumably did the unthinkable.

The Le Poers crated everything and brought the evidence to Richard Ledrede, the Bishop of Ossory. Fears of witchcraft, while not yet as rampant as they would later become, was in the early stages of becoming an Irish obsession. The Catholic Church controlled the country, so Alice was potentially in serious trouble.

Knowing that she had powerful friends (her brother-in-law was the Lord Chancellor of Ireland, and the treasurer was a close friend of her son William), Alice pounced when Bishop Ledrede came to her castle to investigate her for witchcraft. She had him imprisoned in the ancient structure, an act that outraged the church hierarchy. The Dean of St. Patrick's cathedral in Dublin demanded the bishop's release, but Alice stood firm and didn't release her prisoner until 17 days had passed.

Humiliated and furious, Bishop Ledrede enthusiastically led the prosecution against Alice Kyteler. The proceedings represented one of Europe's earliest trials for witchcraft. Alice escaped punishment by fleeing to the home of her brother-in-law, Roger Utlagh, the Lord Chancellor of Ireland. Her servant wasn't so lucky. After confessing under torture that her mistress was a witch who slept with demons, Petronella de Meath was flogged and then burned at the stake on November 3, 1324.

What happened to Alice afterward is not known. By some accounts, she traveled to England and spent the rest of her days there, living to be an old woman. One hundred years later, Gilles de Rais would defy the Catholic Church and suffer a far different fate.

The Maid of Orleans

In 1429, Gilles de Rais was at court when a seventeen-year-old peasant girl named Jeanne, who came from the village of Domrémy, demanded to see the Dauphin. She declared that she had been sent by God to defeat the English, who were now laying siege to Orléans. Although Charles thought she was mad, he was willing to try anything that could bring about a French victory. He ordered Gilles to accompany "the Maid" to face the English forces at Orléans.

Gilles was happy to comply. He found the girl alluring, with her close-cropped hair, boyish figure, and stubborn sense of purpose that rivaled his own.

Jeanne d'Arc (*Library of Congress*)

Jeanne d'Arc, otherwise known as "the Maid of Orléans," was born in 1412 in Domrémy, France, to tenant farmer Jacques d'Arc and his wife Isabelle. At the time of Jeanne's birth, France was still in the throes of yet another conflict in the Hundred Years' War, turning the country's northern regions into a lawless and bloody battleground. In 1415, when she was three, King Henry V of England invaded northern France, shattered the French forces, and won the support of the Burgundians.[10]

The hostilities calmed somewhat with the Treaty of Troyes in 1420, which allowed Henry V to take the French throne as regent for the insane French King Charles VI. The arrangement was that the English king would inherit the throne after Charles died, but both men ended up dying in 1422 and leaving Henry's infant son as king of both countries. French supporters of Charles's son, the future Charles VII, eagerly seized an opportunity to restore a French monarch to the throne.

Around this time, Jeanne began to have mystical visions of St. Michael and St. Catherine proclaiming her as the savior of France and urging her to seek an audience with the Dauphin, Charles. In May, 1428, she cut her hair, dressed in men's clothes, and traveled to Chinon, the

---

[10] The Burgundians were a French political party that formed in the latter half of the Hundred Years' War. Staunchly pro-English, they were opposed by the Armagnacs.

site of the Dauphin's court, where the doubtful but desperate Charles sent her to Orléans to face the English.

Rais was with Jeanne during the battles that raged between May 4 and 7, 1429, when the French troops seized control of the English fortifications. Jeanne was wounded but recovered quickly enough to return to the battlefront and lead a final assault. By mid-June, the English had been successfully routed, and the French people were rejoicing at the thought of their autonomy returning.

After the victory at Orléans, Charles and his procession entered Reims, where he was crowned Charles VII on July 18, 1429. Jeanne was with him, occupying a prominent place at the ceremonies. So was Gilles de Rais.

Rais emerged from the battle at Orléans with nearly as much glory as Jeanne herself. Charles VII made him a Marshal of France, and he was one of four knights who fetched the Holy Ampulla from the Abbey of Saint-Remy to Notre-Dame de Reims for the consecration of Charles VII. He was also awarded the right to add a border of the royal arms, the fleur-de-lys on a blue ground, to his own. The letters patent that authorized the display cited the young nobleman's "high and commendable services." It was an extremely rare honor that was usually accorded to communities instead of individuals.[11]

In the spring of 1430, months after an abortive attempt to take Paris from the enemy, Jeanne went to Compiegne in northern France to confront the Burgundians. Gilles de Rais was not present for this particular campaign. During the skirmish, she was thrown off her horse and captured by the enemy. After several months, she was delivered to the English for 10,000 livers and imprisoned at Rouen, which was the main English stronghold in France.

Gilles de Rais may have planned a rescue. He spent the winter of 1430 at Louviers, which was around fifteen miles from Rouen. He also had an army with him, which was to be expected in occupied Normandy. At one point he was joined by Jean de Dunois, another French military leader, who had also fought alongside Jeanne at the battle of Orléans.

The presence of two French commanders in Louviers is not especially unusual, as the region had been taken from the English the previous year and was in a state of guerrilla warfare. But that winter, an attempt to rescue Jeanne had been initiated by the Armagnacs, a political

---

[11] Benedetti, Jean (1971), Gilles de Rais, p.101

party that supported Charles VII, and one pro-Rais website suggests that Gilles and Dunois were also plotting to liberate her.[12] If they actually tried, the attempt was beaten back like all others that took place during the winter of 1430-31.

Charles VII, whose coronation was largely due to the Maid's battlefield valor, made no attempt to secure her release. Historian Pierre Champion wrote that he threatened to exact vengeance upon captured Burgundian troops for the way the English had treated Jeanne. But otherwise he did nothing when Jeanne, whose actions had actually been against the English military, was turned over to church officials to be tried as a heretic.

Her trial for heresy, witchcraft, and dressing like a man (among other allegations) was initially public, but when Jeanne's responses outdid her accusers, the proceedings went private lest she arouse public sympathy and support. On May 28, 1431, the tribunal found her guilty of heresy and two days later, on May 30, she was brought to the marketplace in Rouen and burned at the stake in front of an estimated 10,000 people. She was nineteen years old.

---

[12] http://gillesderaiswasinnocent.blogspot.ca/

******

Contrary to what some historians have assumed, Gilles de Rais did not retire from the battlefield, disheartened and disillusioned, after Charles VII essentially allowed the English to execute Jeanne. He may have been upset, and even mourned her loss, but he was, above all else, a military leader.

He was present at Beauvais in 1432, when French forces drafted a plan to storm Rouen and kidnap the young English monarch, Henry VI. The scheme came to nothing, but in early August, he got the action he craved when his army encountered the English near Lagny. Rais attacked the besieging forces, who were led by the duke of Bedford, with such skill and enthusiasm that one author described the battle as a repeat of the Orléans victory.

This conflict was different from than his previous ones, however. Rais allowed his men to pillage and plunder in the wake of the battle, something he had never done before.[13] The devastation, which was typical of some military commanders, was abnormal for him.

---

[13] Villalon, L. J. Andrew. *The Hundred Years War (Part III): Further Considerations*, p.164

Gilles' grandfather, Jean de Craon, appears to have sensed a shift in the young noble's behavior, one that worried him. Relations between the two men had been strained for at least three years by that point. In 1429, soon after the birth of his only daughter, Marie, Rais sold his estate in Blaison to an outsider. Craon was furious: after swiftly buying the estate back, he publicly hurled so much abuse at his grandson that local residents still remembered his tirades thirty years later.[14]

A formerly close relationship was now soured. Before dying on November 15, 1432, Craon left his sword and breastplate to Gilles' younger brother René de la Suze. It was a highly public sign of disappointment and dismissal that ultimately broke whatever sense of self-restraint Rais had left.

---

[14] Ibid, p.165

Fall from Grace

Gilles de Rais continued to be active on the military front, but he had clearly changed. In 1434, after assembling troops to liberate the town of Grancy from the Duke of Burgundy, Gilles suddenly refused to actually participate in the battle and relinquished the command of his detachment to his brother, René.

Another atypical act occurred in 1435, when Gilles' cousin, Georges de la Trémoille, asked for his help in a battle against Jean de Luxembourg, who had delivered Jeanne d'Arc into English hands. Rais agreed, but with a fraction of his usual energy, and when his troops protested that they were not getting paid enough, he simply washed his hands of the entire affair.

The military dishonor no longer troubled him like it might have at one time. By that point, he had gradually withdrawn from both public and military life and instead dedicated his energies to the construction of an opulent Chapel of the Holy Innocents, where he officiated in robes he designed himself.

At the time, churches, chapels, sermons, and plays were dedicated to the Holy Innocents all over Europe. Based on verses in Matthew 2: 16-18, the story of the

"Massacre of the Innocents" relates how King Herod ordered the slaughter of all male children in an effort to eliminate his rival as King of the Jews. Then he supposedly took the bloodshed further by killing all children who were two years and under in Bethlehem and the surrounding coasts.

Some books and articles about Gilles de Rais point out that his choice of chapel name reflected a guilty conscience, given the crimes he later died for. While that is possible, it must be pointed out that many French chapels and churches were dedicated to these child saints, and Gilles may have been following the dictates of fashion instead of guilt.

Not long after Jean de Craon died, Rais began selling property to finance an increasingly extravagant lifestyle. His retinue, which accompanied him wherever he traveled, consisted of 25 to 30 people: servants, chaplains, young clerks, singers from his chapel, and children who served as pages. In the chapel itself, he employed a dean, archdeacons, cantors, vicars, a schoolmaster, and more. Occasionally he would be so pleased with one of them that he gave them legacies as well as wages. A choirboy from Poitiers received an annuity worth two hundred livres, and Rais provided a bonus of two hundred crowns for his parents.

By the late winter of 1433 he had sold all his holdings in Maine and every estate in Poitou except those owned by his wife Catherine. Half of the proceeds were spent financing the production of *Le Mistère du Siège d'Orléans*, a theatrical spectacle with more than 20,000 lines of verse, requiring 140 primary actors and 500 extras. It called for six hundred costumes, and Rais directed that after each performance, these costumes be discarded and replaced by new ones. He also ordered and paid for unlimited supplies of food and drink for the spectators who attended the inaugural performance in Orléans on May 8, 1435, and every show thereafter.

It has been suggested that Jean de Craon had served as a moderating influence on his wild-natured grandson, preventing him from committing the deeds that later made him infamous. When the old man died, Gilles gave free rein to his hedonistic impulses.

While he only went into serious decline after 1432, he was already somewhat of a spendthrift, having tried to sell his Blaison estate for unknown reasons in 1429. He was also showing signs of indifference to military honor, evidenced by the failure to stop his men from running rampant at Lagny in August 1432.

Gilles de Rais had never been a paragon of compassion and virtue. He (with full support from his grandfather) had kidnapped his mother-in-law and threatened to drown her. He had also beaten up the royal emissary who had come to ensure that Béatrice de Montjean got her property back. But such Machiavellian violence was common among the nobility, whose primary means of ascension and gain were breaking the backs of others. On the other hand, squandering family money and jeopardizing his military career were definitely not the norm.

Was Gilles de Rais bipolar? During this period of his life, many of his actions could be interpreted as manic: a tendency to show poor judgment, inflated self-esteem or grandiosity, lavish spending sprees, and sexual indiscretions. Some people gripped by mania even see themselves as having superhuman skills and powers. Or could he have incurred a battlefield injury to the head, causing errant behavior to manifest itself later on?

Whatever the cause, 1432 was the beginning of the end for several reasons, one of which was that his earliest alleged victims disappeared.

******

The consensus is that the first child to be murdered by Gilles de Rais was the twelve-year-old son of a man named Jean Jeudon. Sometime in 1432, the Baron's cousins, Gilles de Sillé and Roger de Briqueville, approached a local furrier, Guillaume Hillairet, to whom the boy was apprenticed. They asked if they might briefly employ young Jeudon to take a message to the Rais castle at Machecoul.

Hillairet assented, but when the boy did not return, he questioned the two noblemen. They claimed to know nothing of his whereabouts and suggested that he might have been kidnapped by child stealers at nearby Tiffauges to be made into a page.

The furrier was alarmed but had no cause to doubt the idea. Kidnapping was common in France during the Middle Ages. If a man wanted to marry a woman who refused him, he merely stole her, forced a marriage, and raped her, making the union legal. (A consummated marriage could not be undone.) Landlords also kidnapped children to populate their own villages with young workers and residents.[15]

---

[15] "Medieval Information." Medieval Crimes. Accessed December 2, 2015. http://medieval-castles.org/index.php/medieval_crimes_thieves_burglars_kidnapp.

In the latter instance, tracing the abductor was next to impossible, as the children were usually taken out of their home districts. Only if the missing boy or girl was a member of the nobility was any official effort made to recover them.

Les empocheurs.

Illustration of medieval 'child thieves' (*Author's Collection*)

While young Jeudon's parents were despairing, Jeannot Roussin learned that her nine-year-old son had disappeared. Someone recalled seeing Gilles de Sillé speaking with the boy, but if Rais' cousin was questioned at all, he probably told the same story about an abduction.

Jeanne Edelin, a widow living near the Baron's castle at Machecoul, reported that her eight-year-old son, whom she described as a "comely lad, white of skin and very capable" was gone. Local efforts to find him were still underway when the sons of Mace Sorin and Alexandre Chastelier vanished.

Although these disappearances were not officially tied to Gilles de Rais until eight years later, they did take place at a time when his downward spiral increased in velocity.

******

In June 1435, his alarmed relatives cooperated to prevent Rais from descending into total bankruptcy and dragging the family name down with him. An unsuccessful appeal was made to Pope Eugene IV to denounce the Chapel of the Holy Innocents. His brother, René de la Suze, and his cousin, André de Laval-

Lohéac, also reached out to Charles VII, who obliged in July by issuing a royal edict in Orléans, Tours, Angers, Pouzauges, and Champtocé-sur-Loire. Not only was Gilles de Rais forbidden from selling any more property; those who oversaw his castles were also prohibited from selling them on his behalf, and no subject of the King was allowed to enter into any such sales contract with him.

Predictably, Rais was outraged. When he discovered that a childhood teacher, Michel de Fontenay, had overseen the publication of the King's edict in Champtocé, Rais abducted and imprisoned him at Machecoul. He had no authority to do so, but he didn't care. De Fontenay might have come to the same end as Gilles Meschin had in 1423 had the Bishop and officers from the University in Champtocé not protested until he was released.

Angry and desperate, Rais used his personal property, such as rare books, valuable clothing, and works of art, as security for loans. He also freely disposed of his holdings in Brittany, where the King's edict did not apply, and the reigning Duke, Jean V, ignored the family's pleas to enforce it. He gladly accepted whatever Rais offered to sell him, with the understanding that Rais would be allowed to try buying these holdings back within six years.

These resources brought in some money, but nowhere near the amount Gilles felt he needed to support the lifestyle he wanted. His initial reaction was to retreat under a gloomy cloud of self-pity and depression. Then, when his coffers became dangerously low, he decided on a possible solution that flew in the face of the Catholicism he professed to embrace.

Black magic.

Black Magic

In *The Mammoth Book of True Crime,* Colin Wilson wrote that when Gilles de Rais first went to the Dauphin's court in 1425, he borrowed a book on alchemy from an Angevin knight incarcerated for heresy. The fact that it was illegal enhanced its appeal. Now, a decade later, the beleaguered nobleman thought that alchemy might be the way out of his predicament.

In 1439, he sent a priest in his entourage, Eustache Blanchet, to Italy to find him a genuine magician, someone who could restore his fortune. According to Wilson, he had tried several local prospects who couldn't conjure a bird, let alone piles of gold. In May, Blanchet returned from Florence with a "clerk in minor orders" named François Prelati, a good-looking and charming young man whom Rais was attracted to on sight.

Prelati, who was supposedly a former priest, told his new employer that only Satan could help a mere mortal transmute base metals into gold. To arouse Satan's interest and support, the worst possible crimes had to be dedicated to his name. Children had to be killed, and their hearts, eyes, and sexual organs offered as sacrifices.

A year later Poitou and Henriet Griert told their interrogators (after rounds of heavy torture) that Gilles de Rais quickly kidnapped, raped, and murdered a young peasant boy in honor of the Devil. The body was mutilated and the aforementioned body parts offered up. But when he refused to actually take the final step of selling his soul, Prelati said that he could not participate in the actual conjurations.

These sessions, which took place at Tiffauges, were pure theater. During one of them, Gilles and his cousin Gilles de Sillé heard a deafening series of thumps from inside the room where Prelati was supposedly appealing to the Devil. The two noblemen looked in and found the magician so badly injured he was on the verge of collapse. Asked what had happened, he blurted that the demon Barron had beaten him out of displeasure.

Prelati could just as easily have been hurling himself against the wall to achieve a convincing effect. He was bedridden for several days, and he enjoyed the direct and tender ministrations of his employer the entire time.

Another time, he hurried to tell Rais that Barron had taken mercy on him and empowered him to conjure a pile of gold. Elated, the Baron raced back to the conjuration room, but Prelati got there first. He opened the door, peered in, and yelled that a huge green serpent was guarding the coins. Both men fled, and when they returned, there was no gold, only piles of dust.

To ensure that the nobleman did not lose heart and abandon the experiments, Prelati would tell him wonderful stories and make significant gestures. When Rais spent a month in Bourges during the late summer of 1439, the magician sent him a present supposedly from the Devil himself: black powder on a slate stone. Gilles put the powder in a small silver box and wore it around his neck for days.

Poitou and Griert recalled that after the conjurations and talisman failed to work, Gilles de Rais was so discouraged and depressed that only a return to his murderous debauchery could cheer him up. Sometime in August, the aunt of a young boy named Colin Avril was approached by one of Rais' men (likely Poitou) asking her if they might borrow the child to "show him the house of the Archdeacon of Merles," as she later testified. It was understood that the boy would be given a loaf of bread too.

The aunt must have been uneasy about sending Colin off, because she insisted on accompanying him. But the next day the boy went to the Hotel de la Suze, where he occasionally received bread. Gilles de Rais and his entourage were staying at the hotel at the time.

Colin Avril never came home. Henriet Griert said at his trial that he brought the child to his master, who "had intercourse" with the boy. Colin, he added, was later "killed and burned."

Soon afterward, on the evening of August 26, Poitou brought fifteen-year-old Bernard Le Camus, a good-looking and intelligent teenager, to Rais' new quarters in Bourgneuf. Le Camus, a Breton who was in Bourgneuf to learn French, had caught Poitou's attention at the home of a local resident, where the boy was temporarily staying.

The chambermaid saw Poitou speaking to Le Camus in a way that she must have found suspicious, because afterward she asked Bernard what had been said. The youth shrugged and insisted that Poitou had not told him anything. Then he left and was never seen again.

Poitou said that around this time, he saw Rais put a dead child's hand and heart in a glass, cover it with a linen, and tuck it inside his long sleeve before walking to Prelati's room. The items were apparently offered to

Barron, who failed to appear, so Prelati buried them in sacred soil, close to the castle's chapel.

******

On November 1, All Saint's Day, Eustache Blanchet left Rais' castle at Tiffauges after an argument with one of the Baron's favorite minions, Robin Romulart. The underlying reason was supposedly that he was opposed to the child sacrifices (although apparently not enough to report them). He took rooms at an inn in Montagne.

At the beginning of December, Jean Mercier, castellan[16] of La Roche-sur-Yon, traveled to Montagne and took rooms at the same inn. When the innkeeper asked his guest for news from Nantes and Clisson, Blanchet heard Mercier say that public rumor in those areas accused the Baron de Rais of killing a large number of children so he could write a book using their blood as ink. When the book was finished, the gossips said, Rais could seize all the fortresses he wanted, with no one able to stop him.

The next day, one of Rais' emissaries came to the inn to try and persuade Blanchet to return. The priest refused, insisting that the crimes had to stop because public rumor was mounting against them. When the emissary

---

[16] Governor of a castle

returned to his master without Blanchet, Rais was supposedly so angry that he threw the man into the prison of his castle at Saint-Étienne-de-Mer-Morte.

At the beginning of December, Charles VII's son (the future Louis XI, presently the Dauphin) came to the region of Poitou to put an end to the armed bands of marauders who were ransacking the area. A visit to Gilles de Rais at Tiffauges was on his agenda, so the Baron frantically destroyed all the alchemical ovens in the fortress. After the Dauphin left, Rais went briefly to Brittany, where he enjoyed the hospitality of his old friend Duke Jean, before going to Machecoul in December. It was a move that supposedly proved fatal to two young boys.

******

Two weeks before Christmas, Jeanette Drouet, who resided with her husband and children in Saint-Léger, sent two of her sons, aged seven and ten, to ask for alms at Machecoul. She later testified that she "had heard that Lord de Rais had them distributed there, and that, moreover, the men in that village willingly gave charity."

During the days that followed, several people recalled seeing the boys in the area, but when Madame Drouet went there herself, she found no trace of them.

The hunt for the missing brothers was still underway when Isabeau Hamelin sent two of her boys, aged seven and fifteen, to Machecoul on Christmas Day to buy bread. They never returned. The next day, Prelati and another man, the Marquis de Ceva, came to her door. She recognized both as members of the Baron de Rais' entourage.

Seeing her daughter and another one of her sons, the men asked if they were her only children. Madame Hamelin said there were two more, but she did not mention their disappearance. As they left, she heard one man remark to the other, "Two had come from that house."

Gilles de Laval, baron de Retz. Illustration for L'Histoire de la Magie (1870) by Pierre Christian (Pierre Pitois).

Double Jeopardy

The new year of 1440 was ushered in with blood if Henriet Griert is to be believed. He said that Prelati's friend, the Marquis de Ceva, engaged a teenaged boy, who was supposedly from the Dieppe region and of good family, to serve Prelati as a page. The boy remained at Machecoul two weeks before vanishing. When someone outside the castle asked what had happened to him, Prelati grumbled that the boy had stolen two crowns from him and run away.

Henriet told two versions of the boy's death. In his first forced confession, he said that he murdered the teenager at Machecoul, while in the second he denied remembering who did the killing, as he "wasn't there.... but Gilles abused him just like the others."

Two more boys vanished and were allegedly killed at Machecoul around this time. One was the page of a nobleman named Daussy, while the other was the nephew of a priest who had sent him off to learn to read and write.

Eustache Blanchet, who was finally persuaded to rejoin the Rais household, said that one morning before Easter (March 27), he saw Poitou enter the castle, accompanied by sixteen-year-old Guillaume Le Barbier, son of the village pastry cook. The boy was supposed to serve Jean Péletier, Catherine de Rais' tailor, but soon vanished.

Between March 27 and May 15 (Pentecost), two more boys left their homes, never to be seen again. One was the fifteen-year-old son of a mason from Nantes, whose widow turned the boy over to Poitou after the latter persuaded her. The other was the ten-year-old son of Thomas Aisé and his wife, poor people who sent the boy to Machecoul to beg for alms. Their disappearances added to the rapidly spreading gossip that Gilles de Rais was a fatal force for children.

******

On May 15, 1440, Gilles de Rais made the move that sealed his fate. Earlier, he had sold his estate at Saint-Étienne-de-Mer-Morte to Geoffroy de Ferron, treasurer to the Duke of Brittany. For reasons that have never been made clear, Rais decided to repossess the castle, which had not yet been occupied by Ferron. In the interim, the latter's brother, a priest named Jean de Ferron, was taking care of the premises.

Accompanied by sixty men-at-arms, Rais waited outside the local church, where Jean de Ferron was celebrating High Mass. When it concluded, he ran into the building, a double-sided axe gripped in his hands. He ambushed the bewildered Ferron, yelling, "Ha, ribald! You beat my men, and extorted from them. Come outside the church, or I'll kill you on the spot!"

The shaken priest agreed to surrender the castle to its former owner. Instead of being beaten, he was marched back to the estate and imprisoned in its dungeon.

By barging into a church and forcing Ferron to give up the castle, Gilles de Rais violated both ecclesiastical privilege and the rights of Jean V, the Duke of Brittany. The latter slapped him with a fine of 50,000 gold crowns, but Rais tried to escape paying by moving (and taking Jean de Ferron with him) to Tiffauges, which was outside the Duke's control.

Although the disrespect he had shown the Catholic Church did not appear to trouble the Baron, he soon realized that antagonizing Jean V had not been a wise move, given the fact that the Duke was the only one who would help him liquidate his assets when he needed money. Before setting out on a reconciliation meeting, he ordered Prelati to ask Barron if it was safe to travel into the Duke's territory. Henriet Griert said that three children were killed in a field to ensure a response from the demon.

When Prelati reported that Barron had approved the journey, Rais set out on a mission of reconciliation. He had no idea that his old protector had turned against him. By 1440, Jean V owned most of the Baron's holdings, and if Gilles were convicted of sacrilege (a capital offense) and executed, there was no chance of his retrieving them in six years as per their agreement. The Duke reported the church assault to the Bishop of Nantes and started proceedings for sacrilege, adding a charge of heresy for good measure.

Unaware of the treachery, Gilles de Rais and his party stopped overnight in the town of Vannes after leaving the Duke's household. He wanted to find André Buchet, who had been a choirboy in his entourage in 1434. While there, he was purported to have encountered the ten-year-old son of a local resident named Jean Lavery. Since his present lodging was not private enough for what he had in mind, the boy was taken to another house near the market. There, Poitou said, he was raped, murdered, and decapitated. The body was thrown into the latrines, where the smell of decomposition would be effectively masked.

Rais committed his last canonical murder on August 15. Poitou obtained a young boy by telling the child's mother that he needed a page. He made the story more believable by paying twenty sous for a doublet. According to Poitou, the child was killed and burned.

******

In response to Jean V's allegations and complaint, Jean de Malestroit, the Bishop of Nantes started a private investigation that turned up "evidence" that Gilles de Rais was murdering children and invoking demons. All of his findings were based on public rumor, but for Malestroit, it was enough. On July 29, he published his findings in the form of letters patent and obtained the prosecutorial cooperation of Jean V.

The Duke secured the assistance of his brother Arthur de Richemont, the Constable of France, by promising him two lands that still technically belonged to Gilles de Rais. The Baron had not even been tried yet, but Jean V was apparently so confident of the trial's outcome that he distributed the spoils in advance.

Because he was one of the crown's principal officers, Richemont was empowered to enter Tiffauges, seize it, and free Jean de Ferron. As soon as the Constable entered the estate, Gilles de Sillé and Roger de Briqueville fled for parts unknown. They could see what was coming, even if their master couldn't, and decided to escape rather than go down with him.

On September 13, without his knowledge, Gilles was indicted before the ecclesiastical tribunal of Nantes on charges of sodomy, murdering children, invoking demons, heresy, and offending Divine Majesty. Two days later, he was arrested.

Arrested

Gilles de Rais was at Machecoul when the Duke of Brittany's men, accompanied by a notary public, appeared at its portal with the captain of arms in the lead. When they announced that they were there to arrest him, he gave them no trouble. He probably believed that the arrest was a mere formality in connection with the uproar at St-Etienne-de-Mer-Morte.

Prelati, Blanchet, Poitou, and Henriet were taken into custody too. The latter was not as calm about the situation as his master. On the road to Nantes prison, the terrified servant gave serious thought to cutting his own throat.

******

The trial of Gilles de Rais began on September 19, 1440, on the large upper hall of the castle of La Tour Neve. The proceedings were opened in an ecclesiastical court, which focused on his religious crimes and did not mention the civil charges of sodomy and murder.

The Baron had no idea that the day before, the secular proceedings against him had begun. Authorized by Magistrate Pierre de l'Hôpital and overseen by a cleric,

Jean de Touscheronde, they started off with the testimonies of Peronne Loessart, who had last seen her son in La Roche-Bernard in 1438, and a Port-Launay man named Jamet Brice, who had also lost a son.

Oblivious to this second action, Rais listened as the ecclesiastical prosecutor read out the religious offenses he was being charged with. When he was ordered to appear before the Vice-Inquisitor, Jean Blouyn and the Bishop of Nantes on September 28, he did not protest their authority to try him. He was still confident that a heresy charge could be easily dealt with.

When the 28th rolled around, however, Rais failed to appear as ordered. The heresy proceeding was swiftly joined by the concurrent civil one, as the Bishop and the Vice-Inquisitor listened to a parade of parents and relatives who had lost children in recent years. There were so many of them that the proceedings had to run until October 8 to hear everyone.

The judges also heard the testimonies of Henriet and Poitou, who had been tortured before telling their stories. They had been identified by so many witnesses as being associated with the missing children that the authorities deemed it necessary to apply extra force to get at the "truth."

Poitou said that his master had started killing boys at the Champtocé castle during the lifetime of Jean de Craon. He supplied a date of 1426, although he himself did not enter Rais' service until 1427. Both he and Griert said that boys – and occasionally, girls – would be lured to the castle on some pretext, and once inside the Baron's chamber, be hung from the ceiling on a rope or chain. But before he (or rarely, she) could lose consciousness, they were taken down, stripped, and raped. Once the assault was over, Rais or one of his accomplices would cut their throats or decapitate them.

Sometimes murder was not enough to sate the Baron, who would go on to sexually abuse the child's corpse, sometimes cutting open the stomach and masturbating over the entrails. Afterward, Poitou or Griert would dismember and burn the body in Gilles' fireplace. The ashes were then tossed into the moat, cesspit, and other hiding places.

Poitou recalled that when Gilles' brother, René de la Suze, and cousin came to Machecoul in 1437, Gilles de Sillé and another accomplice removed over forty children's skeletons from the castle. Apparently two had been overlooked and were left in the lower tower. When one of Lord de la Suze's captains asked Poitou and Griert if they knew anything about this, they denied it.[17]

These allegations resulted in the transcript being so lurid that the judges later ordered the worst portions to be stricken from the record.

******

On October 8, 1440, Rais finally made an appearance in the upper hall of La Tour Neve castle. He seemed nonchalant and unconcerned. When the prosecutor read the civil charges against him – murder and sodomy – his genteel demeanor evaporated instantly. Rais exploded in a raging denial and, despite four demands and a threat of excommunication, refused to take an oath.

On October 14, the prosecutor read out the bill of indictment he had prepared. Standing before the Bishop, the Vice-Inquisitor, and several Nantes officials, he formulated the charge as it was laid out in the forty-nine articles of the indictment. According to the lengthy document, the Baron de Rais had started killing children in 1426, and his total victim count was 140 boys and girls. They had been "shamefully tortured" and in the case of the girls, he had disdained their "natural vessel" in favor of sodomizing them. Other crimes included invocations of demons and violating the Church's

---

[17] For whatever reason, this captain was not called to testify.

immunity, which he had done by kidnapping Jean de Ferron.

Interrogated by the Bishop and the Vice-Inquisitor on the forty-nine articles in the indictment, Gilles de Rais became combative. He called his judges simoniacs (those who buy and sell ecclesiastical privileges) and ribalds (those who are vulgar or indecent in speech or language), who had no right to sit in judgement on him.

"I would much prefer," he snarled, "to be hanged by a rope around my neck than respond to such ecclesiastics and judges."

A few minutes after this outburst, a peremptory excommunication took place. He protested, but the Bishop of Nantes stood firm, in view of what the record called "the nature of the case and the cases of this order, and also on account of the monstrous and enormous crimes" brought against the nobleman.

The next day, Rais changed his perspective. The excommunication had greatly upset him, as evidenced by a tearful apology to his judges and his humble acceptance of their authority. He also declared that he was guilty of all the charges against him except invoking of demons, which he suspected that the Church regarded as a more serious crime than murder. At one point, he even collapsed to his knees and begged for the excommunication to be lifted. He seemed so distraught and contrite that the Bishop assented.

Rais' relief must have been palpable. Even when desperate for money, he had refused to sell his soul, and if the ecclesiastical judges wanted to hear a confession in order to lift their excommunication, he would give them one, even if it may not have been true. For by then, he knew that he was doomed.

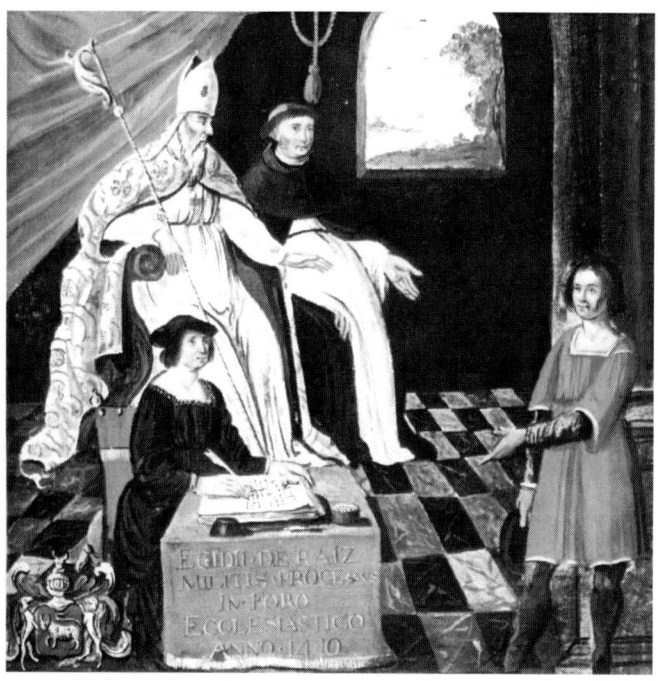

Miniature painting of the interrogation of Gilles de Rais

Guilty

In his confession, which he formally made in court on October 22[18], Rais said that he had started murdering children sometime in 1432 or 1433. He corroborated most of the nauseating testimony supplied by Poitou and Griert. The court record indicates that the Baron spoke "with great contrition of heart and great grief, according as it appeared at first sight, and with a great effusion of tears."

Many times he faced the parents in the audience and begged them to forgive him. They wept too and declared that he was forgiven, a strange response from a group that should have been baying for his blood. Still sobbing, he urged them to watch over their children and ensure they were not "too finely dressed" or lazy.

The next day, October 23, the ecclesiastical court found Rais guilty of heresy, while its secular counterpart declared him guilty of kidnapping and torture and raising armed forces without the Duke of Brittany's permission. The former handed down a sentence of excommunication, which was later lifted after Rais expressed the appropriate level of contrition.

---

[18] After Rais admitted to the charges on 21 October, the court canceled a plan to torture him into confessing.

On October 23 the secular court condemned Poitou and Henriet to death by hanging and burning. The same sentence was passed on Gilles de Rais two days later, on the 25 of October. The Baron, who accepted the punishment humbly, asked for a favor. He wanted to die first, so that Poitou and Henriet could see that he had not gone unpunished.[19]

The court, deeply moved, consented, and told him that instead of being burned afterward, his body could be buried in a church of his choice. The Baron was allowed to make confession, and his request to be buried in the church of the monastery of Notre-Dame des Carmes in Nantes was granted.

---

[19] The other accused men got off relatively lightly. It is not known what Eustache Blanchet's punishment was, but François Prelati was sentenced to life in prison instead of death because there was no proof he had actually participated in any murders. He escaped, but was later caught forging checks and hanged.

The execution of Gilles de Rais

The execution was set for Wednesday 26 October. Because of his high position, Gilles de Rais was granted the comparative mercy of being strangled to death before the flames consumed his body.

At nine o'clock, Gilles and his two convicted accomplices made their way in procession to the place of execution on the Ile de Biesse. Gilles is said to have addressed the crowd with contrite piety and exhorted Henriet and Poitou to die bravely and think only of salvation. Instead of hooting and jeering, which was routine at public executions, people wept and loudly prayed for his soul.

As Rais made his final confession to a friar who had accompanied the execution party, assistant hangmen tested the nooses and their attached chains. When everything was ready, the condemned nobleman ascended the long wooden ladder propped against the gibbet. He paused while the hangman looped the noose tightly around his neck.

In 1440, condemned felons did not wear hoods or blindfolds, so as he stood on the ladder, Gilles de Rais gazed at the staring crowd below, the broad expanse of sky above, and the Nantes countryside all around him. Together, it all comprised his final glimpse of the world.

At eleven o'clock, the brush at the platform was set afire. Gilles either stepped off the ladder voluntarily or was pushed by the hangman. Sometimes the sudden drop broke the victim's neck and caused instant death, but more often death came after slow strangulation. Whatever the case with Rais' execution, he was dead and his body cut down before the flames could reach him. Henriet and Poitou were not so lucky: although hanged first, they were partly burned alive.

Four women identified as "ladies of high rank" claimed the body of Gilles de Rais, which had been cut down after the flames had given it a cursory singeing. As promised, the church permitted his burial in a Catholic cemetery.

Aftermath

Of Catherine de Rais, Rais biographer Jean Benedetti wrote, "It is difficult to imagine that she didn't know about the crimes that the trial of 1440 had succeeded in revealing."

One myth that rapidly became part of Gilles de Rais folklore states that Catherine and her sister discovered blood, a dead child, and other evidence of murder in a Champtocé tower they had been forbidden to enter. The two terrified women alerted their brothers, who led armed forces to the castle and rescued them.

This episode is taken straight from a chapter of *La Barbe Bleue*, a French folktale written by Charles Perrault and published in 1697. In the story, it is the butchered bodies of her predecessors that Bluebeard's wife and her sister discover. Although many commentators suggest that Gilles de Rais was the original Bluebeard, the crimes of the real and mythical personages were too different in terms of victim profile and count, and the gruesome tower discovery by Catherine de Rais never happened.

Whether or not she knew anything about the missing children is impossible to answer now, but what is known is that soon after her husband's execution, she married again, this time to Jean de Vendôme, who became the Duke of Brittany's chamberlain in 1441. Although Gilles had squandered many of his own holdings, Catherine retained Tiffauges, Pouzauges, and the other assets she had brought into the marriage.

For a while, she also controlled the holdings of her daughter, Marie. But the child's possessions were so numerous and valuable that their oversight was passed to Admiral Prégent de Cöetivy, a high-ranking nobleman who was also one of the King's most able advisors. Charles VII actually arranged a marriage between thirteen-year-old Marie and the much older Admiral in the spring of 1442. It was celebrated three years later. The couple had no children at the time of his battlefield death on July 20, 1450.

Marie's second husband was her father's cousin André de Laval-Lohéac, who had worked with René de la Suze to stop Gilles from destroying the family fortune. After their wedding at Vitré in February 1451, he helped her fight to reclaim Champtocé, which her first husband's family insisted was theirs under her marriage contract with the Admiral.

Marie de Rais believed so strongly in her father's innocence that she erected a monument at his execution site years later. It became a place of pilgrimage and remained one for three hundred years, until it was destroyed in the Terror. There, women would pray to the small statue of the Virgin Mary for enough milk to feed their babies. Tradition says that these prayers were answered. It raises an interesting question: If the local people really believed that Gilles de Rais had preyed on and desecrated local children, why was the monument so revered?

Marie de Rais died on November 1, 1457, aged thirty-seven. Because she had no children, her father's legacy passed to his brother René, who officially became Baron de Rais. Being more direct than his cousin or Marie, he seized Champtocé and ignored the indemnification demands made by the Cöetivy family. He died in 1473, leaving everything to his daughter, Jeanne.

******

In January 1443, Gilles de Rais' old benefactor, King Charles VII, sent letters patent to Pierre de l'Hôpital, who had been in charge of the secular investigation, and François I, who had succeeded Jean V as Duke of Brittany. He ordered their appearance before the Parliament of Paris to account for what he saw as the wrongful execution of Gilles de Rais. His anger is detectable in the language used, even centuries later. He refers to the "seizure, arrest, and detention of [the Baron's] person and refusal and denial of justice, and other wrongs and grievances to be declared more plainly at the appropriate time and place, against him and to his prejudice, wrongly, unduly and without reason.... The said late Lord de Rais was condemned and put to death by the said de l'Hôpital, unduly and without reason."

Pierre de l'Hôpital and François I never made the requested appearance, and for some reason the King did not press them. In the letter he insisted that restitution had to be made, and subsequently Gilles de Rais' estates (at least the ones that Jean V had confiscated) were restored to his daughter, Marie.

Like the case with Jeanne D'Arc, Charles got involved too late to do any good. Perhaps the gesture made to Marie was a salve for a guilty conscience.

« 1443 (nouveau style), 3 janvier. – Lettres d'adjornement en cas d'appel, [du procès du mareschal Gilles de Rays], adroissantes au duc [de Bretagne]... – Original en parchemin jadis scellé sur queue simple.

» Charles, par la grâce de Dieu, roy de France, à nostre très chier et très ami nepveu le duc de Bretaigne, salut et dilection.

» Comme feu Gilles, en son vivant seigneur de Rays, mareschal de France, de certaines condempnacions, exploiz, mainmise, arrest et détencion de sa personne et reffus et dené de droit, et autres tors et griefs à déclairer plus à plain en temps et lieu, contre lui et à son préjudice, à tort, indeuement et contre raison, faiz et donnez par feu nostre frère et cousin vostre père, maistre Pierre de Lhospital, soy disant ou portant président de Bretaigne, et autres ses officiers, au prouffit, pourchas, requeste ou instance du procureur de nostredict feu frère et cousin, ou autrement indeuement, eust appelé à nous et nostre court de parlement comme de nulz, et, se aucuns sont ou estaient, comme de faulx et mauvais, iniques et déraisonnables ; après lequel appel, et dedans ung mois après ce que ledit appel fut interjecté, ledict feu seigneur de Rays fut condamné à mort et fait mourir par ledict de Lhospital, indeuement et sans cause, le XXVIJ^e (*sic pour XXVI*) jour du mois d'octobre l'an mil CCCC quarante.

» [...] Si vous enjoignons que vous ayez avec vous audict pour ledict de Lospital, soy portant vostre président de Bretaigne, et autres nos officiers, pour soustenir et deffendre lesdits exploiz, sentences et autres appointements ; les veoir corriger, réparer, amender et mestre au néant se estre le doivent, procéder et avant aller en oultre selon raison. Et vous deffendons que pendant ladicte cause d'appel, contre ne ou préjudice d'icelle ne de nozdictz conseiller et cousine, vous ne eulx actemptez ou innover au contraire, mais tout ce qui fait, actempé ou innové auroit esté, réparez et remectez ou faictes réparer et remectre tantost et sans délay au premier estat et deu.

» Donné à Montalban, le IIJ^e jour de janvier, l'an de grâce mil CCCC quarante et deux, et de nostre règne le XXIe, soubz nostre scel ordonné en absence du grant.

» Par le roy en son conseil. »

CHEVALIER

Conclusion

Was Gilles de Rais guilty? Or did he confess to those terrible crimes to save his soul after being forced to acknowledge that he would never be believed innocent?

The historians who believe that he was guilty insist that the proof against him was overwhelming. He and his accomplices had confessed, and a slew of grieving parents came forward to give evidence against him. But it can also be argued that the confessions had been given under duress, and while Poitou, Henriet, and Prelati had been seen courting victims, Rais can't be tied to them directly.

Today, a good defense lawyer would argue that these procurers had committed the crimes for their own entertainment, and Rais knew nothing about them. He might have been aware that young people were brought to his castles to serve as pages and general servants, but his households were so large that he could never have kept track of their appearances and disappearances even if he had wanted to.

There is no official record of human remains being found at any of Gilles de Rais' castles at any time. Poitou talked about bones being removed from Machecoul prior to the arrival of René de la Suze and the discovery of two skeletons that had been missed, but the captain who allegedly found them never gave evidence at the trial.

It is also a fact that several other children vanished in France during the time that Gilles de Rais was supposedly reveling in young blood, and he could not have been involved in any of their disappearances. They included:

- An eight-year-old orphaned pauper's son (surname Brice), last seen in his home of Saint-Étienne-de-Montluc in February 1439. The Rais household was not in the area, which was a considerable distance north of the Baron's Loire holdings.

- In August 1349, the thirteen-year-old pupil of Jean Toutblanc (also from Saint-Étienne-de-Montluc) vanished. Once more, Gilles de Rais was elsewhere in the country.

- Two months later, in October 1439, two sons of a man named Robin Pavot, who lived near Rennes, attended a fair in Rais. When they didn't come home, their parents made frantic inquiries, and one of their older brothers traveled to neighboring regions, but he could learn nothing. At the time, Rais was at Tiffauges.

To compound the issue, the crowd at the execution site wept and prayed when Gilles de Rais was led out to the gallows. One would think that a vicious child killer would have merited howls and jeers.

The proprietor of a pro-Rais blog[20] made the following observation about the trial judges:

The judges, too, were not as impartial as they ought to have been in a capital case. Jean de Malestroit had engaged in numerous business deals with the accused, buying his estates at knockdown prices. He was the cousin of Jean V, Duke of Brittany, who had also illegally bought properties from his vassal, including the strategic border castles of Champtocé and Ingrandes. These fortified castles were vital to Brittany´s defense, and Jean V´s father had coveted them before him. Although the Duke finally obtained them, when Gilles´ finances were on the verge of collapse and he could no longer hold on to them, they were sold on condition that Gilles could repurchase them within six years if he wished. Neither Jean V nor de Malestroit was willing to risk such an eventuality.

---

[20] http://gillesderaiswasinnocent.blogspot.ca/

The question of guilt or innocence has proved to be so troubling over the centuries that in 1992, Gilles de Rais was retried in an official process of rehabilitation.[21] A French arbitration court consisting of lawyers, historians, politicians, and writers was assembled to determine whether there was sufficient evidence to prove he might have been framed.

Historian Gilbert Prouteau, who led the campaign, said, "The case for Gilles de Rais's innocence is very strong.... No child's corpse was ever found at his castle at Tiffauges, and he appears to have confessed to escape excommunication....The accusations appear to be false charges made up by powerful rival lords to benefit from the confiscation of his lands."

Former Justice Minister Michel Crepeau seemed to agree. He said that the trial's true motivation appeared to be political.

The court studied the minutes of the Baron's trial at the hands of Jean de Malestroit and heard arguments that he was the victim of circumstantial evidence. The presiding judge, Henri Juramy, later said that the primary motive was to ascertain whether French history had

---

[21] http://www.theguardian.com/theguardian/2013/jun/17/bluebeard-gilles-de-rais-france

been deliberately damaged by the original condemnation.

Some French newspapers reported that the Roman Catholic Church, unwilling to reopen a ruling by the Inquisition, accused Freemasons of being behind the creation of the arbitration court.[22]

When the hearing concluded, Juramy declared that Gilles de Rais was not guilty of murder. The ruling spawned a documentary called *Gilles de Rais ou la Gueule du loup*, which was narrated by Prouteau.

Two lobbies protested the acquittal. One was the Catholic Church. The other was the local residents living in the vicinity of Tiffauges, Machecoul, and Champtocé. For them, vindicating Gilles de Rais posed a serious threat to their livelihood, given the number of tourists who visited the ruined castles every year. Tiffauges guide Georges Gautier declared, "We're not interested in reopening the affair."[23]

---

[22] Riding, Alan. "Bluebeard Has His Day in Court: Not Guilty." The New York Times. November 16, 1992. Accessed December 6, 2015. http://www.nytimes.com/1992/11/17/world/bluebeard-has-his-day-in-court-not-guilty.html.

[23] Ibid

Because the trial and verdict took place before the Internet exploded, the acquittal is not generally known, and most history and serial killer sites continue to refer to Gilles de Rais as the "original Bluebeard" whose guilt is beyond question. The gruesome details of his alleged crimes are too shocking and morbidly appealing for many true crime writers and fans to even want him to be innocent.

At the same time, his complete innocence doesn't seem possible. Even if the crimes were the private perversions of Gilles de Sillé, Poitou, or Henriet Griert, could they really have taken place at Tiffauges, Machecoul, and Champtocé without Rais knowing or suspecting anything?

The debate will go on for a while yet, for after all this time, all anyone can do is conjecture. When a person's crimes are as sensational and iconic as those attributed to Gilles de Rais, his guilt or innocence will always be like beauty: in the eye of the beholder.

Bibliography

Bataille, Georges. *The Trial of Gilles De Rais*. Los Angeles: Amok, 1991.

Benedetti, Jean. *Gilles De Rais*. New York: Stein and Day, 1972.

MacCulloch, Diarmaid. *A History of Christianity*. Penguin Books, 2010.

Villalon, L. J. Andrew. *The Hundred Years War (Part III): Further Considerations.* Brill, 2013.

Wolf, Leonard. *Bluebeard, the Life and Crimes of Gilles De Rais*. New York, N.Y.: C.N. Potter, 1980.

Photography Credits

Gilles de Rais – painting – cover and text
"Gillesderais1835" by Éloi Firmin Féron - Agence photo de la Réunion des musées nationaux RMN - http://www.photo.rmn.fr/archive/94-052333-2C6NU0018VE9.html. Licensed under Public Domain via Commons - https://commons.wikimedia.org/wiki/File:Gillesderais1835.jpg#/media/File:Gillesderais1835.jpg

De Rais'seal
« Guy-de-laval-retz-sceau » par Paul de Farcy (1840-1918) — http://gallica.bnf.fr/ark:/12148/bpt6k55162550/f113.image.r. Sous licence Domaine public via Wikimedia Commons - https://commons.wikimedia.org/wiki/File:Guy-de-laval-retz-sceau.jpg#/media/File:Guy-de-laval-retz-sceau.jpg

Illustration from l'Histoire de la Magie
Gilles de Laval, baron de Retz. Illustration for l'Histoire de la Magie (1870) by Pierre Christian (Pierre Pitois). « Gilles De Rais » par Émile Bayard — http://www.allposters.com/-sp/Gilles-De-Rais-Posters_i1862404_.htm. Sous licence Domaine public via Wikimedia Commons https://commons.wikimedia.org/wiki/File:Gilles_De_Rais.jpg#/media/File:Gilles_De_Rais.jpg

Jeanne d'Arc
« Joan of arc miniature graded » par Derived from original commons upload at which is now in the history version: 01:39, 13. 8. 2005Colour-graded to reveal more detail using GIMP software "curves" tool. Sous licence Domaine public via Wikimedia Commons https://commons.wikimedia.org/wiki/File:Joan_of_arc_miniature_graded.jpg#/media/File:Joan_of_arc_miniature_graded.jpg

Gilles de Rais murdering children
"Gilles de Rais murdering children" by Jean Antoine Valentin Foulquier - First Gallery. Licensed under Public Domain via Commons https://commons.wikimedia.org/wiki/File:Gilles_de_Rais_murdering_children.jpg#/media/File:Gilles_de_Rais_murdering_children.jpg

Miniature painting of the interrogation of Gilles de Rais during his trial
« Gilles-de-rais-tribunal » par Anonyme — Bibliothèque nationale de France (BnF). Sous licence Domaine public via Wikimedia Commons https://commons.wikimedia.org/wiki/File:Gilles-de-rais-tribunal.jpg#/media/File:Gilles-de-rais-tribunal.jpg

The execution of Gilles de Rais
« Exécution Gilles de Rais » par Inconnu — BNF RC-A-03432 FRANCAIS 23836 - Procès de Gilles de Rais. Sous licence Domaine public via Wikimedia Commons https://commons.wikimedia.org/wiki/File:Ex%C3%A9cution_Gilles_de_Rais.png#/media/File:Ex%C3%A9cution_Gilles_de_Rais.png

More Books from Jack Smith

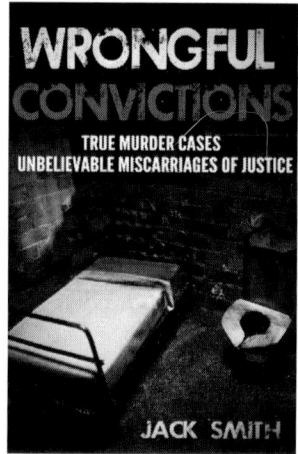

Made in United States
North Haven, CT
30 September 2025